DAVID COLBERT

10
DAYS

ANNE FRANK

D1508724

ALADDIN PAPERBACKS

NEW YORK LONDON TORONTO SYDNEY

❦ ALADDIN PAPERBACKS • An imprint of Simon & Schuster Children's Publishing Division • 1230 Avenue of the Americas, New York, NY 10020 • Text copyright © 2008 by David Colbert • The photographs in this book are under copyright and are reprinted here with permission of the owners. All rights reserved. Full copyright notices appear on pages 151 to 152 of this book, which constitute an extension of this copyright page. • All rights reserved, including the right of reproduction in whole or in part in any form. • ALADDIN PAPERBACKS and related logo are registered trademarks of Simon & Schuster, Inc. • Cover designed by Karin Paprocki • Interior designed by David Colbert • Special thanks to Julie Baker for her important contributions to this book. • The text of this book was set in Perpetua. • Manufactured in the United States of America • First Aladdin Paperbacks edition September 2008 • 10 9 8 7 6 5 4 3 2 1 • Library of Congress Control Number 2008920645 • ISBN-13: 978-1-4169-6445-2 • ISBN-10: 1-4169-6445-2

I come from a people who gave the Ten Commandments to the world. Time has come to strengthen them by three additional ones, which we ought to adopt and commit ourselves to: Thou shall not be a perpetrator; thou shall not be a victim; and thou shall never, but never, be a bystander.

—Yehuda Bauer, professor of Holocaust Studies at the Hebrew University of Jerusalem, in a speech to the German Bundestag

CONTENTS

AFF/AFH/Getty Images

© Mark Squires

USHMM

USHMM

DAY 8:
SEPTEMBER 5, 1944
SEPARATED

Anne loses her father's protection and enters the dark world of the Nazis' most notorious camp.

DAY 9:
OCTOBER 7, 1944
SECRETS AND LIES

The twisted cruelty of the Germans' hatred leads to horrors beyond anything Anne has imagined.

DAY 10:
MARCH 1945
"WE HAVE OUR PEACE"

Sent to a new camp, where an epidemic rages, Anne tries to comfort her dying sister.

AFTERWORD:
JULY 19, 1945
LEGACY

The lone survivor of the Frank family is handed a precious and powerful legacy: Anne's diary.

INTRODUCTION

The short life of an ordinary schoolgirl may seem to be an unlikely subject for a biography. Yet when we read about Anne Frank, we defy what Nazi Germany hoped to achieve. The Holocaust was meant to be nameless—the Nazis tattooed numbers on most of their victims instead. Some of the world's first large computers, sold to the Nazis by the American company IBM, literally reduced the victims to old-style computer punch cards. So the personal story of every Holocaust victim is an act of defiance simply because it's personal.

It's easy to quote statistics: six million Jews murdered—90 percent of the Jewish population of Poland, Germany, and other European countries. More than three million Poles, Slavs, Communists, Socialists, pacifist Christians, Gypsies (Roma), homosexuals, disabled, and people of African descent bring the total murdered to perhaps eleven million.

However, those statistics, shocking as they are, say nothing about the experience. You can only memorize numbers like those; you can't feel them. The story of a single life can tell you more about the Holocaust than any statistic, no matter how large. Without stories like Anne's, the Holocaust would be too vast to comprehend.

Anne's life began just as the Nazis rose to power and ended just as the Nazis were defeated. She knew almost every part of the experience: what it felt like to have Nazi soldiers invade her neighborhood, to be branded as less than human, to live in hiding, to have a family separated into different death camps, and to be a prisoner of people who took a bizarre pleasure in cruelty. Like millions of others, she knew what it felt like to be murdered, slowly, by Nazi Germany.

Yet she also knew what it felt like to laugh during those horrible times. She watched movies with friends. She had crushes. She tried to get out of schoolwork. She had all the usual arguments with her mother that any girl her age might have. Anne understood that even any normal day under Nazi rule, even a dull day, was a victory for her and her family.

Anne lived approximately 5,748 days. (Because of conditions in her concentration camp, her exact date of death remains unknown.) Still, because of the events of the ten days that follow, she left her mark. These days changed her world—and yours.

① ② ③ ④ ⑤ ⑥ ⑦

⑧ ⑨ → ⑩ ← 1 2 3

4 5 6 7 8 9 10 1 2

3 4 5 6 7 8 9 10 1 2

3 4 5 6 7 8 9 10

ONE TWO THREE FOUR FIVE SIX

DAY 1

ONE

MAY 15,

1940

SURRENDER

Amsterdam, Netherlands.

In less than a month, Anne will be eleven years old. She wishes she were older, like her sister, Margot, who's already fourteen. Margot's the quiet one. Anne has the big personality: talkative, happy, dramatic, and usually the center of attention. *I'm older than her in a lot of ways*, Anne thinks.

For the last few days, however, Anne's been quiet. Her parents have been whispering to each other nervously. They listen to the radio for news reports, but wait until Anne and Margot are out of the room before talking about the broadcast. Her father, Otto, with whom she usually has fun, is distant. Today Anne's parents have barely spoken to each other. When Anne tried to talk to Margot about plans for a birthday party, Margot ignored her.

A few minutes ago Mr. Frank peeled back a piece of the blackout paper that he taped against the windows several months ago, when citizens of the Netherlands were told to keep their cities dark at night so warplanes couldn't find them. Now he's staring out the window, not speaking with anyone. For the last half hour, a humming sound from outside has been steadily growing louder. *Is that music?* Anne wonders.

She has never seen her father nervous like this. She adores him—unlike her feelings for her mother, Edith, with whom she often argues. He's usually calm and strong, qualities she admires and wishes she had in herself. Now he almost seems afraid. Seeing him like this is making her nervous too.

Europe's borders in 1939. The arrow shows the Netherlands.

She knows why he's worried. The Netherlands has surrendered to the German army, and troops are now marching into Amsterdam. Still, to Anne, Nazis are just villains in radio news stories. She never expected to see one. She knows her family left Germany when the Nazis took over the country in 1933, but she was just four years old then. The Netherlands is what she knows. Although it's a neighbor of Germany, it's a very different place. In the Netherlands, Anne has always felt safe. Most of the Dutch people, as citizens

Germany bombed the Dutch city of Rotterdam to force surrender.
This stone church had been surrounded by buildings.

of the Netherlands are known, think Nazism is ridiculous. Those who agree with the violent views of Adolf Hitler stay quiet about it. The Dutch are proud of having stayed neutral during the First World War. Anne has often heard her father say that the Netherlands will remain neutral if Hitler leads Germany to war again.

Today, for the first time, she realizes her father can be wrong about something like that. His mistake was thinking that the Netherlands could defend itself against Germany. The German army is much too strong. It has more troops and tanks and warplanes than any army in the world. No country has been able to resist it yet. It has already invaded Austria, Poland, and Czechoslovakia. Now it's right outside.

Mrs. Frank walks to the window. She almost seems to be hiding behind Mr. Frank as she peers out.

"I should have known this would happen," Mr. Frank says to her. "I should have sent the girls to England." Anne doesn't know it, but a few weeks earlier one of Mr. Frank's cousins, who lives in England, had told him to send Anne and Margot to her for safety. Her parents couldn't bring themselves to do it.

Mrs. Frank doesn't reply. She seems to agree: *He should have known.*

BLAME GAME

Unlike some of his Dutch neighbors, Otto Frank has seen for himself the insane frenzy of the Nazis. Eight years earlier, when Hitler came to power in Germany, he had seen the huge demonstrations. He'd watched as Hitler gave himself the power to ignore the German constitution. He saw Hitler describe imaginary threats to frighten the public and win its approval for outrageous laws, such as abolishing any political parties except the Nazi Party. He saw how quickly the German people responded to Hitler's racist message: Germans are superior to other people; Germany's loss in the First

World War, and the extreme poverty and unemployment that followed, were the fault of a conspiracy of foreigners and Jews.

Hitler's Nazi government called for a boycott of Jewish businesses and doctors. It fired civil servants who were Jewish or who had even one Jewish grandparent. Laws were passed to prevent Jewish children from going to school with non-Jews. Jews were fired from universities. The government found several ways

Five-year-old Anne, her sister Margot, and two friends whose families also escaped Germany have a tea party with their dolls. Left to right: Anne, Ellen Weinberger, Margot, and Gabrielle Kahn.

to take property from Jews. Gangs, some of them organized by the Nazi Party, beat up Jews for fun.

Otto also saw the feeble response of some Jews to these attacks. Their idea of resistance was to insist they were loyal Germans. Some of them proudly wore the medals they had received when serving in the German army during the First World War. Otto, who had also served in the German army, knew the madness of the Nazi mobs could not be fought with reasonable arguments. People who are passionate about racism are like people who still believe that the world is flat or that the sun revolves around the earth: They're frightened by ideas or opinions that don't fit their view of the world. A thoughtful argument enrages them simply because it's thoughtful. It reminds them of the ignorance that makes them weak.

Weakness is something the Nazis can't admit. They're determined to stamp out any sign of it, even when it's imaginary. Within a few years, they quietly execute at least seventy thousand—and likely many more—Germans with disabilities, many of them children, simply for falling short of the Nazi ideal. They sterilize others to prevent them from having more "genetically unfit" children.

MOB RULE

Within months of Hitler's rise to power in 1932, Otto arranges for the move to the Netherlands. With the help of family and friends, he establishes a local branch of his company. (It makes pectin, a chemical used in jelly and industrial gels.) From the Netherlands, he continues to follow the rise of the Nazis.

In 1938, about five years after the Franks move to Amsterdam, Nazi violence against Jews in Germany reaches a new level with an event called *Kristallnacht* ("Crystal Night"), also known in English as "The Night of Broken Glass." With the approval of the government, synagogues and Jewish businesses throughout

A Nazi rally in Germany

Germany and Austria are destroyed by mobs. Windows are shattered; whole buildings are burned. After a few days of these riots, the government arrests thirty thousand Jewish men and boys and sends them to concentration camps.

Hitler then sets his sights on small countries near Germany. Other countries, like France and Great Britain, let him have his way. Throughout Europe, citizens remain furious with politicians and military leaders about the First World War, in which tens of millions of soldiers and civilians died. During and just after that war, monarchies were overthrown in Russia, Germany, Finland, and Hungary. Civil war broke out in several countries. European leaders are not willing to risk more lives—or their own careers. When Hitler takes part of Czechoslovakia, the prime minister of Great Britain, Neville Chamberlain, calls the fight "a quarrel in a far-away country between people of whom we know nothing."

Germany's official racism spreads quickly.

THE ENEMY WITHIN

Anne can hear the music clearly now. It's a German military song.

Five days ago the loud drone of airplanes flying low overhead woke the Franks in the middle of the night. Soon they heard explosions. No one dared peek through the windows, but the Franks, like all their neighbors, turned on the radio to hear the news: *The German invasion of the Netherlands has begun. Bombers have hit Amsterdam's airport. German paratroopers are already deep inside the Netherlands' borders.* The next day Anne, Margot, and all their friends were kept home. Adults visited shops to stock up on food. That was difficult. The Netherlands has been rationing its food for months, because Germany's invasions of neighboring countries have hurt the economy. Some of Anne's friends had even tried to hoard candy, in case it disappeared from stores. (They quickly ate through their supply!)

According to radio reports, the Dutch were putting up a strong resistance. Mr. Frank believed the Nazis would be stopped, or at least delayed long enough for France and Britain to come to the rescue. Because he believed it, Anne believed it too.

It didn't happen. The French army tried to help, but was unsuccessful. The British didn't come at all.

Then came the shocking news report that Queen

Wilhelmina had fled the country, escaping to London. Many Dutch people felt abandoned.

Finally, German planes bomb the important port city of Rotterdam. The Dutch government decides it must surrender. The Germans can't be stopped.

Now German soldiers are parading through the Franks' neighborhood, where many Jews live. Anne feels a shiver. The danger is starting to become real to her. She can't see the soldiers, but she can see the look on her father's face. She knows what it means. A few years later she would write in her diary, "After May 1940 the good times were few and far between." **❶**

1 2 3 4 5 6 7
8 9 → 10 ←

1 2 3
4 5 6 7 8 9 10 1 2
3 4 5 6 7 8 9 10 1 2
3 4 5 6 7 8 9 10

ONE TWO THREE FOUR FIVE SIX

DAY

TWO

2

APRIL 29,
1942

"JOOD"

Amsterdam.

A nne is daydreaming about her thirteenth birthday, just six weeks away. The past year has been difficult. She and Margot now attend one of the new schools established by the Nazis to keep Jewish children apart from other children. She didn't like the new school at first, mostly because it was more strict than her old one, but now she's having fun more often than not.

One change, however, still bothers her a lot.

She rarely sees old friends who aren't Jewish. The Germans have been successful in segregating people. The parents of one of her old friends have even joined the Dutch version of the Nazi Party. Her friend is now a member of the Dutch version of the party's youth group, the Youth Storm. The girl is just going along with what her parents want, but it's still strange for Anne to catch a glimpse of her old friend on the street in the Youth Storm's military-style uniform.

Many of the Dutch, both Jews and non-Jews, have resisted the German laws. A year earlier, when Germans began to arrest and imprison Jews for no apparent reason, people all over the country went on strike for a day. In stores, factories, and restaurants people suddenly stopped working. Truck drivers and streetcar drivers stopped their vehicles.

The Germans are quick to retaliate against such protests. Many people have been taken away to Nazi labor camps. It's as if they've disappeared.

DAYSTARS

The Hague, Netherlands.

I n a luxurious office in the Netherlands' capital city, a German officer is standing in front
of a full-length mirror. He's amusing himself
by holding a large yellow Star of David, a traditional
Jewish symbol, over the medals on his uniform. The
star has the word "Jood," Dutch for "Jew,"
printed on it in a typeface that mimics
the shape of Hebrew letters. He rubs the
cloth star to feel the quality of the fabric.
Strong, he thinks. He's impressed.

The officer is Ferdinand Hugo aus der
Fünten. He runs the Netherlands' division of the SS,
a police force that also acts as Hitler's personal army.
(SS is an abbreviation for *Schutzstaffel*, which in German means "protective squadron.") SS members are
selected as Hitler's ideal racial type: Christian and
Northern European—what the Nazis refer to as

"Aryan." (SS members and their wives must prove their Aryan ancestry back to the year 1700.) The SS is deeply loyal to Hitler. Even the regular German military fears the SS.

The SS carries out Hitler's policies against Jews, such as removing Jewish students like Anne from regular schools and taking Jewish property. Today aus der Fünten is introducing a rule that's meant to help the police identify Jews. From now on Jews must sew the yellow star onto their clothes.

This idea didn't originate with the Nazis. Laws requiring Jews to wear special badges or clothes go back centuries. In England, a law passed in the year 1275 required a cloth badge shaped like the stone tablets of the Ten Commandments. In the early Christian era, both Christians and Jews were branded. However, the practice has been regarded as barbaric since the Middle Ages.

There's a knock at the office door. A soldier leads in two members of the Jewish Council, a committee

A government poster from Germany, where the word for "Jew" is "Jude." It reads, "Whoever wears this symbol is an enemy of our people."

of Jewish citizens. The Council, which was established by the Germans, is supposed to communicate and carry out Nazi regulations. Its members don't like their task. They've agreed because they think they can soften the blow of the Nazi policies. They're mistaken.

Aus der Fünten explains the new regulation and shows them the sample Star of David he'd been playing with a few minutes earlier. They're speechless, but aus der Fünten is cold to their shock. He likes this

The Nazis enforced boundaries of Jewish zones in the major cities they occupied. The sign announces in German and Dutch the entry to the Jewish zone of Amsterdam.

new regulation. He wants them to get started quickly.

Using the example of Jews in Germany and Poland, where similar badges are already required, German bureaucrats have methodically counted the number of coats, jackets, or dresses a Dutch Jew might own, and made a star for each one. For the Netherlands' population of about 150,000 Jews, they have delivered 569,355 stars to aus der Fünten.

"It's the Council's responsibility to distribute them," aus der Fünten says. "You have three days."

"Three days! All over the country?!"

"Of course. Also, it will be your responsibility to collect the fee. Each badge will cost four cents and one clothes ration coupon."

"We must pay for them too?"

"Naturally. You'll be wearing them. Now, I've drawn up a contract for the Council to sign, confirming the deadline and your responsibility for the fees."

COMMANDMENTS

Amsterdam.

Later that evening, when she's doing her homework, Anne sees her father taking the clothes ration books from a drawer in a small table in the kitchen. *A new dress!* she thinks.

Anne has an eye for fashion. Margot is happy with anything, but Anne is particular about her clothes. In fact, she's already seen some things she'd love for her upcoming birthday.

By the next evening she'll be disappointed. Angry too. Her father will tell her not to worry. Along with distributing the stars, the Jewish Council offers a hopeful message that's whispered among the Jews of the Netherlands: *We must bide our time. The Germans have taken on too much, fighting the Russians and the Americans. The war will be over in a month or two. Then we'll be free.*

Desperate for good news, many Dutch Jews believe it. It's far from reality. In the next few months aus der Fünten will enforce many new regulations against Jews. Anne will later list in her diary the ones she remembers most:

> . . . *Jews were required to turn in their bicycles; Jews were forbidden to use trams; Jews were forbidden to ride in cars, even their own; Jews*

*Every outfit had to include a badge, even wedding dresses
and formal clothes. The couple in this photo, Mr. and Mrs.
Salomon Schrijver, who married in Amsterdam in 1942, were
killed in the Sobibor death camp in Poland on July 9, 1943.*

were required to do their shopping between
3:00 and 5:00 p.m.; Jews were required to
frequent only Jewish-owned barbershops and
beauty parlors; Jews were forbidden to be out on
the streets between 8:00 p.m. and 6:00 a.m.;
Jews were forbidden to attend theaters, movies
or any other forms of entertainment; Jews were
forbidden to use swimming pools, tennis courts,
hockey fields or any other athletic fields; Jews
were forbidden to go rowing; Jews were forbidden
to take part in any athletic activity in public;
Jews were forbidden to sit in their gardens or
those of their friends after 8:00 p.m.; Jews were
forbidden to visit Christians in their homes;
Jews were required to attend Jewish schools . . .

Yet while the Germans make daily life difficult and even dangerous, Anne notices signs of human kindness from many non-Jews: Thousands of them are wearing the yellow stars. This protest stops only when the

Nazis arrest the protesters and imprison them in work camps for several weeks.

By then the protest has already reminded Anne and many other Dutch Jews that the Nazis haven't yet succeeded in separating them from their neighbors. Soon, some of those neighbors will come to the rescue of the Franks. ❷

① ② ③ ④ ⑤ ⑥ ⑦

⑧ ⑨ → ⑩ ←

1 2 3

4 5 6 7 8 9 10 1 2

3 4 5 6 7 8 9 10 **12**

3 4 5 6 7 8 9 10

ONE TWO **THREE** FOUR FIVE SIX

DAY 3

JULY 6,
1942

THREE

THE VANISHING

Amsterdam. 6:00 A.M.

Despite the early hour, the whole Frank family is already dressed. With nervous whispers, Mrs. Frank is ordering Anne and Margot to get their last things together: schoolbooks, extra clothes, toothbrushes. The Franks are about to disappear.

There's a knock—a very soft knock—at the apartment door. Everyone jumps. When Mr. Frank goes to answer it, Mrs. Frank instinctively pushes Anne and

Margot behind her and toward a back room.

Everyone exhales when they see it's only Miep Gies, Mr. Frank's secretary.

Mrs. Frank leads Margot to the door, but doesn't quite let go of her. Mr. Frank examines his daughter, who's dressed in a heavy overcoat despite the summer weather. Frowning, he tugs at the yellow Star of David on the coat. Mrs. Frank rushes over with scissors. She and Margot remove it. Their hands are shaking.

"We'll see you very soon," Mr. Frank says to Margot. "Now go."

Breaking the law, the Franks have kept one of their bicycles, which Jews are forbidden to own. Now, while Anne and her parents watch from the window, Margot and Miep pedal away in rainy darkness.

Turning to Anne, Mrs. Frank points to a small stack of clothing nearby. Anne adds layers to the clothes she's already wearing. Two vests. Three pairs of pants. A dress. A skirt. A wool cardigan. Coat. Head scarf. She swelters under so many things, but

Mrs. Frank says it's necessary. If they carry luggage, people will know what they're doing. Under the new Nazi laws, Jews aren't even allowed to move to new apartments. Shopping bags are all they can risk. Anne worries the added bulk will attract attention, but Mrs. Frank is in no mood for argument.

While her parents finish their preparations to leave, Anne gets a small satchel from her bedroom. She puts her diary, hair curlers, handkerchiefs, a comb, schoolbooks, and a few old letters inside it. "I put in the craziest things with the idea that we were going into hiding, but I'm not sorry, memories mean more to me than dresses."

Mr. Frank scrawls a note on a piece of paper and leaves it where he is sure it will be found by anyone who visits the apartment looking for them. The note suggests that the Franks have left the Netherlands for Switzerland. If the police believe they have sneaked out of the country, Mr. Frank reasons, no one will bother to conduct a search.

An hour and a half later Anne follows her parents out of their home and into the pouring rain. Jews are forbidden to use any kind of transportation in Amsterdam so the Franks must walk, each struggling under the weight of extra clothing and overstuffed bags. "We got sympathetic looks from people on their way to work. You could see by their faces how sorry they were they couldn't offer us a lift; the gaudy yellow star spoke for itself."

MAN WITH A PLAN

Mr. Frank knew this day would come. He understood that each new rule the Germans imposed on Dutch Jews was like the slow tightening of a noose. The planning for this morning began months ago.

He had already tried to get his family out of the Netherlands, but, because of the war, traveling was difficult and required special permits that were impossible to get. Few countries welcomed Jews anyway. A few years earlier the German government thought of a clever way of preventing criticism by other countries: It put about a thousand Jews on a boat, the SS *St. Louis*, and allowed the passengers to ask other countries for asylum from German persecution. First Cuba, then the United States, and then Canada refused to take in the passengers. President Franklin Roosevelt made the decision for the United States. Initially willing to take in some passengers, he was threatened by other powerful politicians that they'd stop supporting him if he opened the country to Jewish refugees. In Canada the decision was made by the prime minister and one of his top aides, who said that when it came to allowing Jews into the country, "None is too many." (The passengers were eventually allowed into Britain, France, and Belgium, thanks in part to unofficial help from the United States.)

Although Mrs. Frank's brothers lived in the United

States and Mr. Frank had the help of an influential friend, the U.S. government wouldn't issue travel visas for the family. He knew other Jews had the same trouble trying to enter the United States, Britain, and Canada. That's when Mr. Frank decided they would all go into hiding. The company he runs has some unused rooms set apart from the main offices. The entrance to them can be hidden. There's enough space for the family to stay together.

He told his plan to one of his Jewish employees, Hermann van Pels, whose family could join the Franks. (In Anne's diary, the van Pels family is given the name "van Daan.") Van Pels agreed it would work. However, it would require asking four other employees for help. That would be a lot to ask. Anyone caught hiding a Jew can be executed.

Without hesitating, all four agreed to help. (Along with Miep were Johannes Kleiman, Victor Kugler, and Bep Voskuijl. Some of their relatives later joined the effort.) In the months that followed, the extra rooms—what the company calls "the annex"—were secretly prepared. Household items and canned food were smuggled past the German police. Windows were covered.

In early summer Mr. Frank explained the plan to Margot and Anne. The idea, he said, is to slip away in the middle of July. Then something forced them to disappear suddenly, ten days earlier than planned.

Just yesterday a policeman arrived at the Franks' apartment with a letter for Margot. It says she must report to the SS offices today. She'll be sent to a labor camp in Germany. The letter is vague about the details, but behind it is a very specific and horrible plan. The SS is enslaving Jews from all over Europe to work in German factories. It has set a goal of several hundred Jews a day. Margot, being sixteen years old and therefore considered well fit for work, was among the first to receive an official notice. It makes the camp sound like a normal place, with proper housing and food, but the Franks certainly weren't fooled.

That evening, in a panic, the Franks made their final rushed arrangements. Miep and her husband, Jan, stopped by to pick up some last things to be smuggled into the office hideaway. They make the plan for Miep to pick up Margot very early.

THE SECRET ANNEX

The steady rain continues until Anne and her parents reach Mr. Frank's office. As planned, it's still early, and the employees haven't arrived. Mr. Frank leads Anne and his wife through the main office and storeroom, to an unmarked door in the rear of the building. "No one would ever guess that there would be so many rooms hidden behind that plain door painted gray," Anne writes later in her diary. "There's a little step in front of the door and then you are inside." She calls their new home the "secret annex."

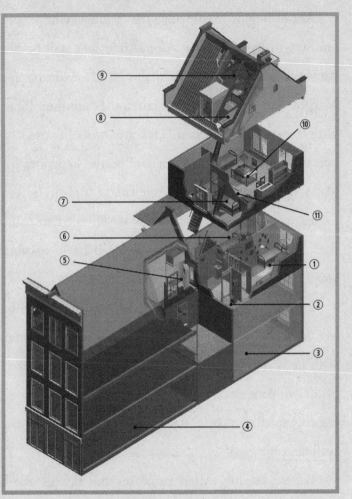

The secret annex

① *Anne's room (later shared)* ② *Bathroom* ③ *and* ④ *Company offices and storage* ⑤ *Hidden entrance* ⑥ *Bedroom of Mr. and Mrs. Frank and Margot* ⑦ *Peter's room* ⑧ *Attic* ⑨ *Loft* ⑩ *Living room during the day, bedroom of Mr. and Mrs. van Pels* ⑪ *Kitchen*

Anne begins exploring the rooms where her family will live. The first room Anne sees will be her parents' bedroom. Another tiny room will be for Margot and herself. Up a staircase is another floor, with a makeshift kitchen. This area will be used by everyone during the day, but will be the bedroom for Mr. van Pels and his wife, Auguste, at night. The van Pelses, who are coming in a few days, will also bring their fifteen-year-old son, Peter. He'll be in another small room.

Looking around the rooms, Anne is impressed by her father's preparations. He has stocked the annex with beds, tables, chairs, cans of vegetables, and bags of dried peas and beans. He even brought Anne's photographs of movie stars for her to paste on the wall near her bed.

Before leaving, Miep promises the Franks she'll deliver fresh groceries soon. She has obtained illegal food-ration cards for the Franks and the van Pelses, and she knows of a grocer who won't question why she and her husband need supplies for so many people. Miep assures Anne she'll also bring movie magazines when she can get them. Miep seems to have a special understanding of what the Franks are feeling. Like them, she came to the Netherlands as a refugee. She's from Vienna, Austria. In 1920, when she was eleven—just a couple of years younger than Anne is now—Europe had extreme food shortages. She was close to starving when a charity helped her parents send her to live with

AFF/AFH/Getty Images

Miep Gies

sponsors in the Netherlands. The family that took her in was loving and generous, as were their friends and her schoolmates. In time she decided the Netherlands was home.

Mr. and Mrs. van Pels

Anne and her father immediately begin unpacking boxes, organizing supplies, and covering the windows with scraps of fabric they manage to find. Curtains will keep passersby from seeing them during the day, but heavy cardboard will be needed on the windows at night to keep light from shining through. Mrs. Frank and Margot have simply collapsed with exhaustion from being nervous.

Although Anne suddenly feels very alone, the Franks are not the only Jews in hiding. Other Jewish families throughout Europe have chosen to disappear instead of reporting to the slave labor camps. Between 1942 and 1943, more than twenty thousand Jews in the Netherlands hide in attics, basements, and spare rooms tucked in forgotten corners of old houses. Their lives are being saved by the courage of people like the ones helping the Franks. Unfortunately, very few families are able to stay together as the Franks and the van Pelses will do.

After he and Anne hang the makeshift curtains

Peter van Pels

*Although the Franks are hiding near the heart of Amsterdam,
the building with the secret annex attracts little attention.
Its plain facade blends in with a row of similar buildings.
The annex is in the rear of the building.*

protectively over the windows, Mr. Frank sits down to create a list of rules his family and the van Pelses will follow during the time they remain hidden.

Noise, Mr. Frank tells the family, is the enemy. During business hours, everyone must be silent. Some of the workers in the office below have no idea that anyone is hiding in the building. Flushing the toilet and running the sink will have to wait until the end of each workday because of the sound of water in the pipes.

Mr. Frank also creates a daily schedule. The workday below starts at 8:30 a.m.; therefore, everyone in the secret annex must wake up by seven o'clock and finish their morning routine quickly. Each will have a turn in the bathroom and help push beds out of the way to make room for tables and chairs. The noisy task will be completed prior to the arrival of employees in the office. Breakfast will be from nine until nine-thirty, but it must be prepared and eaten as quietly as possible. After that, he announces to Anne's disappointment, there'll be schoolwork.

Inside Anne's room in the secret annex

Downstairs, the workers are already arriving for the day. Anne and Margot pull out their schoolbooks and try to read. It's difficult for Anne to keep her attention on her work.

At twelve-thirty, the office closes so the workers can go home for lunch (a common practice in Europe). Anne still can't make much noise—people on the street could hear—but she can at least relax a little. At two o'clock the workers return, then four more silent hours pass before Miep comes upstairs to say the workers have gone home. Anne dances around the room. Finally, she can make a *little* noise!

At nine o'clock that evening chairs and tables are pushed aside, and beds are pulled out for sleeping. The annex has only cold water, so hot water for baths is brought up from below. By ten o'clock everyone is in bed, but Anne lies awake long into the night. She hears voices and footsteps in the street below. Something scurries across the floor in the darkness.

She feels lucky that her father thought of creating this hideaway, but she doesn't feel safe in it. ❸

1 2 3 4 5 6 7

8 9 → 10 ← 1 2 3

4 5 6 7 8 9 10 1 2

3 4 5 6 7 8 9 10 **12**

3 4 5 6 7 8 9 10

ONE TWO THREE **FOUR** FIVE SIX

DAY

FOUR

4

MARCH 28,

1944

"DEAR KITTY"

Secret Annex. 5:30 P.M.

As the last of the office staff leaves the building, the occupants of the secret annex scramble to Otto Frank's former office and its precious radio. It's their lifeline.

They keep the volume barely loud enough to hear. First they listen to the English-language news from the British Broadcasting Corporation in London. From the BBC, they've heard reports of massive battles raging across Europe and Asia. They also hear reports about life for civilians, including Jews like themselves. While German radio stations repeat the government's lies that Jews are being treated well, British reporters testify that vast numbers of Jews are being enslaved or murdered. After the BBC news, the residents of the annex listen to a daily report in Dutch, transmitted by the Dutch government in exile in Great Britain. The Germans forbid the people of the Netherlands to listen to these broadcasts, but all over the country people are listening anyway. There's usually a message from Queen Wilhelmina, whom the Dutch have forgiven for fleeing just before the country surrendered to Germany. She's absolute in her hatred of the Nazis.

Tonight, however, instead of the queen, the residents of the annex hear the voice of Gerrit Bolkestein, the minister of education, art and science. For a moment Anne is disappointed. Then she hears what he has to say. His message has more meaning to her than anything else she's heard on the broadcast.

"History cannot be written on the basis of official

Queen Wilhelmina and her daughter Juliana,
who succeeded her after the war.

decisions and documents alone," he says. What are needed are "ordinary documents—a diary, letters from a worker in Germany, a collection of sermons given by a parson or a priest." Not until then, he concludes, will the world know of the struggle for freedom by the Dutch people.

As he says the word "diary," all eyes turn to Anne.

HOORAY FOR HOLLYWOOD

Two years earlier: It's still a few months before she and her family go into hiding. Anne is thinking about her upcoming thirteenth birthday. Leaving nothing to chance, she shows her father what she wants most: She points to a red-and-white checked autograph book in the window of a book and stationery shop. For a few years now she's been writing in school notebooks whenever she has a spare moment. One of her dreams is to become a professional writer. On the morning of her birthday the new diary is wrapped and waiting for her on the breakfast table.

There's little sign of the famous writer Anne hopes to become in the first diary entries. After an initial entry expressing the hope that she can confide in the diary, and that she looks to it for comfort and support, the earliest entries include some snippy observations of her classmates, a few put-downs of boys she doesn't like, and a little gushing over the ones she does. An avid moviegoer, she longs to have a dog she can name after Rin Tin Tin, the dog hero in several Hollywood films she has seen. As if she does not trust the diary, the early entries are surface observations and more about others than herself.

A few months later she is more trusting of sharing

Anne has written: "This is how I wish I looked all the time. Then maybe I would have a chance to go to Hollywood."

Anne's first diary

her feelings. She realizes her family respects her desire for privacy concerning what she chooses to write. She's able to confide in her diary that, despite a circle of friends and family, she feels completely alone in the world. When the Frank family is forced to go into hiding, the first item Anne packs is her diary.

Because she's writing in something meant only for signatures and short notes, the pages are often too

short to contain everything she wants to write. Sometimes she writes on scraps of paper that Miep sneaks
out of the office, and pastes these into her pages.
Other times she'll skip certain days and then return
to them when she is certain of what she wants to say.

When she fills the first diary, which has only a
little over a hundred pages on which to write, she
continues writing in a series of notebooks and various
colored papers from Miep.

Inside the diary

Anne Frank Fonds-Basel/Anne Frank House-Amsterdam/Getty Images

Anne at age 13

A few months after going into hiding, she rereads one of her favorite books, Cissy van Marxveldt's *Joop ter Heul*, which is written in the form of letters from a bouncy, fun-loving narrator—the Joop of the title, with whom Anne identifies—to a group of friends. Anne decides to use that form for her diary.

As she becomes more and more a prisoner of the annex, her writing becomes more introspective. The exuberant, optimistic young girl who once dreamed of being an ice-skating queen or a Hollywood star has given way to someone wise about the world. Despite being challenged by the bleak existence she and her family face each day, her skill as a writer continues to grow. Her observations become sharper; her expressions become clearer. She writes short stories and fairy tales. Her writing begins to take on a voice that's distinctly hers. She even imagines sending her work to a publisher, but she knows that even with a pseudonym that risk is out of the question.

"I KNOW THAT I CAN WRITE"

Tonight the radio broadcast calling for diaries has thrilled her. *Published!* But then she wonders, *Is it good enough?* She barely hears the rest of the broadcast, because she's already thinking about ways to make her diary into a book. By the time everyone has tumbled back into the secret annex, she has composed in her head some of the revisions. Soon she'll go back over everything in the original diary and the notebooks that followed it, giving it a strong, purposeful form. She sharpens its focus, addressing each revised entry to a single friend, "Kitty."

Each evening she'll gather her pages and her diaries and carefully place them in her father's old briefcase. Everyone in the annex knows to respect her need for her writing to be private. The briefcase seems a safe place to store her work.

As she rewrites, a complete picture of life under the Nazis takes shape. She decides that her diary can be the basis of a novel she will write, which she calls *The Secret Annex*, a title she is sure will not only attract publishers but Hollywood as well.

She's conscious of her own growth and yet full of the self-doubt that writers before and after her have often felt. "I *know* that I can write," she says, "a couple of my stories are good, my descriptions of the secret annex are humorous, there's a lot in my diary that speaks, but whether I have talent remains to be seen." ❹

BREAK-IN

Secret Annex. 9:30 P.M.

Strange sounds are coming from the office below the secret annex, which should be empty now. It's the evening of Easter Sunday. The staff left Friday afternoon for the three-day Easter weekend. Could it be Miep or Mr. Kugler? No, they would have said they were coming. The police? No, police would not bother to soften their footsteps. Anne's father tiptoes toward the entryway of the secret annex to investigate.

The moving bookcase that hides the secret annex

The gray door that separated the annex from the office has been replaced with a movable bookcase that better hides the entryway. Mr. Frank swings it open a crack. He listens for a moment and then opens it farther and slips silently into the office. The other men follow him. For what seems like several minutes, the four stand motionless in the dark, waiting for more sounds from below. Maybe the prowler has left the building. Maybe he is still there in the darkness somewhere, waiting and listening.

From within the annex, Anne hears stairs creak as the men cautiously descend into the main office. She hears no sound or movement anywhere else in the building.

Suddenly, the silence is broken by a shout and a loud bang.

Mr. Frank and Mr. van Pels run back up the stairs and into the annex. "Lights out!" Anne's father orders the women. "We expect the police!"

"What happened?" Anne asks. Her father rushes downstairs again without answering.

Several minutes later all the men return to the annex and latch the bookcase closed behind them. Then Mr. Frank finally tells the women what happened. Burglars were inside the office, he says. Mr. van Pels shouted "Police!" and they fled. Unfortunately, there were two other people strolling along the canal in front of the building when the commotion occurred, and one of them shone a light in through the warehouse door.

Mr. Frank fears someone, maybe even the burglar, will figure out that people are hiding in the building. The Nazis reward people who turn in Jews. Anne, like everyone in the annex, knows that capture means a prison camp. If they're discovered by regular Dutch police, there's a small chance that they can bribe their way out of trouble, but they'll have no chance with German military policemen.

As the annex residents consider the worst, Anne's diary comes up. What if the police find it? They'll discover who has been helping the fugitives hide. They'll learn anything Anne might have written about the residents' friends and relatives, some of whom are hiding elsewhere.

"Burn it," someone suggests.

Oh, not my diary, Anne thinks. *If my diary goes, I go too*. Fortunately, the subject is dropped.

The nervous families take turns watching out Peter's window and listening for warning signs that someone is coming. Time seems to pass slowly. Then, a little more than an hour after the break-in, every-one hears someone climbing the stairs. Whoever it is seems to be heading directly for the entry to the annex. Then a flashlight beam shines through the small gap under the movable bookcase. The person on the other side isn't one of the helpers.

Now we are lost, Anne thinks.

The intruder rattles the bookcase, trying to find how to open it. Anne holds her breath. More rattling, harder now. Then there's a sound—a tin can, or some-thing like it, falls to the floor on the intruder's side of the entryway.

Moments later, his footsteps start again, this time headed away from the annex and down the stairway. But the thin thread of light remains. Has the intruder forgotten his flashlight? Will he return for it? Is some-one still out there?

There's nothing to do now but wait. Sleep is impossible. Everyone retreats into the back rooms of the annex. Making the night worse, everyone in the annex has been sick. It's the worst night Anne can remember. "During that night," she later wrote in her diary, "I really felt that I had to die, I waited for the police, I was prepared. . . ."

As she lies in the darkness, listening and waiting with the others, Anne counts the months they have lived within the walls of the secret annex. The Franks and the van Pelses have been hiding for twenty-one months. Dr. Fritz Pfeffer, a middle-aged dentist from Germany who joined them after asking Miep for help, has been there for seventeen. (Dr. Pfeffer is called "Albert Dussel" in the diary.)

To pass that time, they read books Miep brought them, wrote poems, and celebrated special occasions with handmade presents. Mostly, though, they're silent. Noise is dangerous.

"When someone comes in from outside," Anne writes, "with the wind in their clothes and the cold on their faces, then I could bury my head in the blankets to stop myself thinking: 'When will we be granted the privilege of smelling fresh air?' Believe me, if you have been shut up for a year and a half, it can get too much for you some days. Cycling, dancing, whistling, looking out into the world, feeling young, to know that I'm free—that's what I long for. . . ."

Anne quietly asks Margot what she will do as soon as the war is over and they are allowed to return home again. Margot says she wants to take a long, hot bath. Peter hears them and says he wants to go to a movie. Mrs. van Pels longs for a taste of ice cream cake. Anne just wants to go outside.

Anne also plans what she will write in her diary after this frightening night is over. She wishes she had a friend with whom she could share her fears and worries. She and her mother bicker. Her father still views her as a child. Margot is quiet and stays to herself. Mr. and Mrs. van Pels are always fighting. Anne doesn't like Dr. Pfeffer, who she thinks is too old and too impatient to understand her. Even Peter van Pels, whom Anne has some romantic feelings for, doesn't strike her as a worthy confidante. The only place she feels safe expressing her feelings is in her diary.

Just after seven o'clock the next morning, more footsteps are heard. "It's the police!" someone whispers. No one moves.

As before, the steps progress quickly through the building and up the stairs. They come to a stop in front of the bookcase.

This time there's a knock.

Two heartbeats later, there's a familiar whistle. Miep! They all breathe at once. Miep is here. That's her signal that all is well. It's not the police!

Relief overwhelms Anne as Miep and her husband, Jan, hurry into the secret annex. Anne throws herself into Miep's arms and begins crying. They are safe, Miep assures them after learning what has happened. Their hiding place in the annex is still safe.

The night's terrifying events, however, convince the Franks, the van Pelses, and Dr. Pfeffer that drastic changes must be made in their daily routine to ensure their continued safety. The families agree not to go downstairs anymore, even when they feel certain they are alone in the building. They'll be more careful about propping windows open for fresh air, even on the most uncomfortably warm evenings. All sounds are far too dangerous now, so they vow not to flush the toilet late at night. In her diary, she writes, "We have been pointedly reminded that we are in hiding, that we are Jews in chains, chained to one spot, without any rights, with a thousand duties. Sometime this terrible war will be over. Surely the time will come when we are people again, and not just Jews!" ⑤

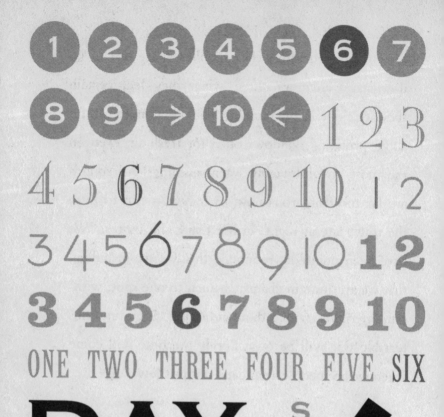

ONE TWO THREE FOUR FIVE SIX

DAY is SIX

AUGUST 4, 1944

CAUGHT

Secret Annex. 11:20 A.M.

Anne closes her notebook and stretches her arms above her head. She has spent most of the morning on math problems her father assigned. He is still upstairs teaching Peter the day's English lesson, though, so she takes her diary off the shelf instead.

Glancing up to make sure her mother has not noticed, Anne thumbs through the diary's handwritten pages to the back. She comes across an entry written two months earlier and happily reads again the wonderful news she was able to report on that day:

> Tuesday, 6 June, 1944
>
> Dear Kitty,
>
> "This is D-day," came the announcement over
> the English news and quite rightly, "this
> is the day." The invasion has begun!
>
> Great commotion in the "secret annex"! Would
> the long-awaited liberation that has been talked
> of so much, but which still seems too wonderful,
> too much like a fairy tale, ever come true? Could
> we be granted victory this year, 1944? We don't
> know yet, but hope is revived within us; it gives
> us fresh courage, and makes us strong again.
> Oh, Kitty, the best part of the invasion is that
> I have the feeling that friends are approaching.
> We have been oppressed by those terrible Germans
> for so long, they have had their knives so at our
> throats, that the thought of friends and delivery

fills us with confidence! . . . I may yet be able

to go back to school in September or October.

Yours, Anne

Everyone listened to the radio that evening, joyful and smiling as reporters told how soldiers from the Allied forces—the United States, Britain, Canada, and other countries—were battling Germans along the coastline of Normandy, France. They're so close, Margot had said happily. It's only a matter of time now, Mrs. Frank agreed.

Her parents and the van Pelses had danced and laughed all evening, as loud as they dared, and their joy remained long after Anne's fifteenth birthday, six days later. Even Dr. Pfeffer was happier than she had ever known him to be.

Miep brought newspapers so Anne and the others could continue to follow the progress of the Allied forces. Mr. Frank found a map of Western Europe in one of them, and he cut it out and attached it to the wall in the annex. Every time the BBC or newspapers report a new location of fighting between the Allies and the Germans, Mr. Frank places a pin on the map. The pins have been gradually approaching the Netherlands, which means the Allies are winning. Anne is sure it will be only a few more weeks before the Allies drive Hitler's soldiers out of Amsterdam.

For now, it's back to less exciting thoughts: She knows her father will expect to see some of the math problems completed when he and Peter finish for lunch. First, however, she flips through the last few pages before closing her diary, the entry she wrote on July 15, 1944, catches her attention: ". . . in spite of everything, I still believe that people are really good at heart."

I'll keep that part in when I revise the section tonight, she promises herself, and then reaches for her math book.

11:55 A.M.

While Anne thinks about her diary and works on the math problems her father has assigned, Miep is in the office, finishing some paperwork before the lunch break.

A stranger enters the building and walks straight to her desk. From his pocket, he draws a gun and points it at her. He orders her not to speak and not to move. She can tell at once that he's not a robber. He's a plainclothes police officer.

The company manager, Mr. Kugler, hearing the unfamiliar voice, comes out of his office to investigate. The policeman tells them that someone just called the police station to report that Jews are hiding here. He motions Mr. Kugler back inside his office, and then follows him. The office door closes firmly behind them.

Miep desperately wants to warn Mr. Frank and

the others, to somehow get them down the stairs and away to safety. She knows that's impossible. Besides, there's nowhere for the families to go.

Maybe he won't find the annex, she thinks. She wonders if he'll question her closely, and reminds herself of the lies she has practiced. Suddenly she remembers the illegal food ration cards she uses for the annex residents. With shaking hands, she removes the cards from her purse and jams them in a desk drawer.

Unaware of what has just happened, her husband Jan arrives. She whispers to him that something is wrong and passes him the illegal ration cards. He nods in understanding, hides the cards in his clothing, and immediately leaves. Along with helping the Franks, he's a member of a secret group that organizes a lot of activities against the Germans. Much as he might want to stand by Miep right now, he has a responsibility to avoid being caught.

Within minutes, several policemen arrive. One is wearing the uniform of the Gestapo, a German police force under the command of the SS. Mr. Kugler is ordered to lead their way up the stairs toward the entrance to the secret annex. One of the policemen uses the office telephone to call for a police van.

USHMM

The first policeman to enter the secret annex was Karl Josef Silberbauer.

Miep knows for certain that the fugitives have been found.

A few moments later she hears the officers open the movable bookcase that covers the annex entrance.

Inside the annex, Anne, Margot, and Mrs. Frank are the first to see the policemen. There's no need for the officers to tell the women not to move. They're paralyzed with fear.

Officers spread throughout the annex, bringing all the annex residents into the front room at gunpoint.

Revealing the cheap thuggery that defines so much of the Nazi attitude toward non-Germans, the police immediately demand the families' valuables.

Victor Kugler, one of the helpers, arrested along with the fugitives

Mr. Frank points to a small wooden chest in a nearby closet. One of the officers opens the box and dumps its contents onto the floor. Then he opens Mr. Frank's briefcase and does the same. Anne's diary falls from it and lands among the scattered papers. The officers sort through the items, collecting anything that might be of value. They ignore the diary.

The prisoners are escorted to the police van waiting outside the building. Mr. Kugler and Mr. Kleiman are also arrested. Miep is safe for now, only because one of the senior officers is Austrian. When he learns she's Austrian too, he gives her a break.

After the automobile pulls away, Miep and Bep go into the annex. The Franks' cupboard drawers have been yanked open and the floor is littered with books and papers the police left behind. Miep sees Anne's diary and some loose papers with Anne's handwriting on the floor. She picks them up, along with a photograph album, a few books, and a small fabric bag embroidered with the initials "AF." Back downstairs, she gently places Anne's diary, papers, bag, and photographs into her desk drawer. She decides to keep them for Anne, refusing to accept the possibility that the Franks may never return.

AFF/AFH/Getty Images

Johannes Kleiman, another helper

Meanwhile, the prisoners are driven to Gestapo headquarters in the southern section of Amsterdam and locked in a cell. Mr. Frank whispers to Mr. Kleiman, who risked his life to help the Franks: "You can't imagine how I feel, Kleiman. To think that you are sitting here among us, that we are to blame. . . ."

"Don't give it another thought," Mr. Kleiman says. "It was up to me, and I wouldn't have done it any differently."

The two non-Jews, Mr. Kleiman and Mr. Kugler, are soon taken away to be questioned separately.

The captured fugitives spend their first night away from the secret annex in a Gestapo jail cell—still together. It has been twenty-five months since the morning Miep and Margot pedaled to the annex from the Franks' apartment. ❻

*Heinrich Himmler, head of the SS and the man in charge
of the concentration camps. His goal was the murder of all
Jews. He believed it was a noble task and pitied himself for
witnessing the suffering of his victims. He told his men that
they should feel the same—that they were the true victims.*

1 2 3 4 5 6 7

8 9 → 10 ←

1 2 3
4 5 6 7 8 9 10 1 2
3 4 5 6 7 8 9 10 **12**
3 4 5 6 7 8 9 10

ONE TWO THREE FOUR FIVE SIX

DAY SEVEN 7

AUGUST 8,
1944

WESTERBORK

Amsterdam. 9:00 A.M.

The Franks, the van Pelses, and Dr. Pfeffer have been under arrest for four days. Today they're being sent to Westerbork, the work camp Margot was supposed to go to more than two years earlier—and where, by now, the rest of them would have already been sent if they hadn't hid in the secret annex.

Anne knows their situation is serious, but she can't deny that she's enjoying the ride in the police van just for the motion of it—the familiar bounce of hard tires against Amsterdam's cobblestones. She's adopted the attitude of her father, who's still most concerned about the people who are in trouble for helping the fugitive Jews. Although he has no illusions that life in the work camp will be easy, he has reminded Anne and Margot that the Allies are close to defeating the Germans. The time in the secret annex wasn't for nothing. It kept them safe through most of the war, and now they'll see the final victory.

At Amsterdam's main train station, the prisoners are escorted by police to a train platform. Most of the Dutch people in the station look away. Some are ashamed; others want to spare the prisoners any embarrassment. Everyone knows what's happening.

On the train, Anne scoots close to her father and watches from her window as the train chugs out of the station. Within minutes the city is gone and the Dutch countryside stretches for miles in every direction. It has been a long time since Anne has seen cows and sheep and meadows of green grass and brightly colored flowers. The sheer beauty of nature fills her with optimism once more.

"We were together," Mr. Frank will later remember about the day, "and had been given a little food for the journey. We knew where we were bound, but in spite of that it was almost as if we were once more going travelling, or having an outing, and we were actually cheerful. The war was so far advanced that we could begin to place a little hope in luck."

"CRIMINAL JEWS"

Camp Westerbork. 3:20 P.M.

Late in the afternoon the train arrives at Westerbork labor camp, in the northeastern region of the Netherlands. The station is in the center of the camp, which is surrounded by a barbed-wire fence topped with spikes. Anne sees soldiers with machine guns inside the watchtowers above the fencing. Westerbork is a "transit camp" where Jewish people are held temporarily before being transferred to other Nazi camps. Nearly one hundred thousand Jews have passed through its gates in the months before the Franks and their friends arrive. As many as sixteen thousand people are imprisoned in the dirty, crowded camp at any given time.

The Westerbork transit camp was built around a railway line.

The train stops, and its bolted doors are opened swiftly by Westerbork's prison guards. They wear soldiers' uniforms and carry guns. Their faces are serious and tense. An impatient voice barks orders for everyone to get off the train. Another shouts for the Jewish prisoners to assemble outside: Men are separated to the right and women to the left. Damp wind presses against Anne's face and rushes through her thin clothes as she steps to the ground. The air is fresh and cool compared to the stuffiness of the train's cabin, though, and she takes a deep breath in gratitude.

One guard orders the new arrivals to proceed to "registration." Men and boys line up in front of one row of desks. Women and girls go to another. The lines are long and movement is slow.

Anne stands in a line with her mother, sister, and Mrs. van Pels. When it's her turn, she tells the woman behind the desk her name, date of birth, nationality, and where she had lived in Amsterdam. The woman types the information onto a small blue-green card

Dutch Jews on their way to Westerbork

without looking up from her typewriter. Then she files the card in a large box behind hundreds of other cards she has typed for previous prisoners.

The women are then taken to another building where guards order them to remove all of their clothing and shoes. Anne and the others stand naked in line to have their hair cut and to be checked for lice. Then they're examined by a German doctor. The doctor scribbles notes about each woman's health on another small card and it goes into another large box.

Each woman is issued wooden clogs and a dark blue prison uniform to replace the clothing that was taken from her. The uniforms given to Anne, Margot, Mrs. Frank, and Mrs. van Pels also have red patches sewn on them so everyone at the camp will know they are "Criminal Jews." They've been assigned this special criminal designation because they illegally hid from the Nazis instead of turning themselves in for deportation. "Criminal Jews" are given the most dangerous jobs at Camp Westerbork, receive less food than other inmates each day, and are not permitted to have toiletry items like soap.

Students and teachers at a Westerbork school

Anne's first work day will start tomorrow at 5:00 a.m. in the camp's battery department. Margot, Mrs. Frank, and Mrs. van Pels will also work there. They will each be given a small chisel tool and will spend the day taking apart batteries, removing the carbon rods inside the metal covers, and scraping out the chemicals inside. Mrs. Frank and Mrs. van Pels are not sure what the chemical is called or what the Germans will use it for, but they hear it will burn their hands and their eyes and their lungs.

After the prisoners' paperwork is complete and their duties in the camp have been made clear, the guards allow them to familiarize themselves with their new surroundings. Anne and Margot walk to the battery building where they are scheduled to work. The girls peek inside and see rows and rows of women, all in dark blue uniforms, working side by side at long tables. Each table is covered with batteries and battery parts. A few of the women are having quiet conversations, but their eyes never leave the batteries and chisels their hands are holding. Anne notices that some kind of brown chemical is leaking from the batteries and staining the women's hands, faces, and clothing. Her nose begins to itch from the strange smell the brown chemical emits into the air. Several women cough as they breathe it in. A German guard yells at the women to work faster.

HOPE SPRINGS ETERNAL

7:00 P.M.

The "Criminal Jews" are not allowed to live together as families at Camp Westerbork. Mr. Frank and the other men of the secret annex are assigned to an all-male building in a separate section of the camp away from the one where Anne and the others will be staying.

The families are allowed to reunite for a few minutes each evening, however. The Franks and the van

Pelses gather to talk about the people they have met and the rumors they have heard during their first day as prisoners of Westerbork. They share news from and about people they knew in Amsterdam who they've seen today at Westerbork.

Mr. Frank then tells them of a rumor going around the camp. American military forces, Mr. Frank says, are near the French capital, Paris, which the Germans have held for four years. If the Americans can take control of France from the Germans, they'll be able to free the Netherlands.

That's the kind of rumor Anne wants to believe as she struggles to sleep next to her mother and Margot that night in a room with three hundred other women prisoners. **❼**

Americans troops march down the Champs-Élysées in Paris, just a few weeks after the residents of the annex were caught. It would take several more months for the Netherlands to be liberated.

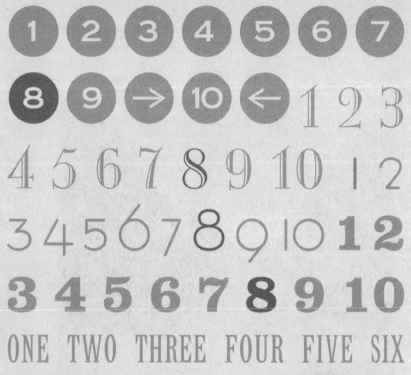

ONE TWO THREE FOUR FIVE SIX

DAY

ONE TWO THREE FOUR FIVE SIX

8

E
I G H
T

SEPTEMBER 5,
1944

SEPARATED

German-Occupied Poland. 8:15 P.M.

After a month in Westerbork, Anne and her family are being transferred by train to a new camp. The train has been traveling for three nights and two days. Anne doesn't know its exact destination.

This train is nothing like the one that took the Franks to Westerbork. It's not even built for humans. The Franks are huddled inside a dirty, crowded cattle car with seventy other prisoners. There are no seats, no bathrooms. The passengers are being treated like animals, which is how the Germans think of them.

Three nights ago, at Westerbork, just after the workday ended, guards ordered all of the prisoners to line up in rows outside the barracks. Then the guards took turns reading a long list of 1,019 names in alphabetical order from a sheet of paper. The members of the Frank family, the van Pels family, and Dr. Pfeffer were among those whose names were announced. They were ordered to return to their barracks and pack suitcases for a long journey.

SS troops

Prisoners being loaded onto a train leaving Westerbork

Just before dawn the next morning, several SS troops arrived to supervise the loading of the families into the train's windowless boxcars. Anne knows all about the SS now. She's seen why they have a reputation for torture and brutality, and noticed that the regular camp guards are frightened of them.

Anne kept her head down as she passed by the SS troops. Inside the boxcar, she saw the Nazis had scattered some straw over the floorboards and placed two large buckets in one corner: One held water for drinking and the other was empty. Anne realized the empty one was for her and the other prisoners to use as a community toilet. There were also two narrow openings built near the ceiling of the compartment; Margot told her the slats were designed to allow circulation of air for livestock. After loading the prisoners, the SS guards locked the boxcar doors.

"I think of darkness when I think of that train trip," a fellow passenger will later say. "Too many people. Not enough space. Luggage. No space to lie down. Three days of sitting. Every now and again standing. We had no idea where we were going, where we would stop, and how long it would take."

East, someone had said, we're headed to the east. To Poland, someone said.

That's not good, Anne knows. The Allies are in the other direction, to the west. She and her family are being moved away from the army that's coming to free them.

The train is now slowly rolling to a stop. Anne

hears German guards speaking outside. The metal boxcar doors are flung open from the outside and bright lights momentarily blind the frightened prisoners. Anne is on the opposite side of the cattle car, crouched behind dozens of people, and cannot see what's happening at first. What she hears, though, is absolutely terrifying.

German voices shout: "Move! Move! Everybody out! Get Moving!" The alarmed prisoners rush to comply.

Mothers clasp the hands of their children and fathers grab the families' small suitcases. Everyone presses forward toward the powerful light. Their legs are stiff from days of entrapment, their stomachs ache from hunger, and their clothing is soaked with urine and sweat. Anne holds tight to her father's hand, determined not to be separated from him in the chaos.

When they get to the opening of the boxcar, though, she hesitates before hopping down to the

Arrival at Auschwitz-Birkenau

ramp below. The floodlights illuminate everything in sight, but Anne sees only the SS soldiers who surround the platform. Some hold machine guns. Others carry leather whips. A few grip the leashes of attack dogs. All of the soldiers are yelling: "Hurry up! Leave your luggage! Get moving!"

While Mr. Frank helps Anne's mother and sister climb out of the train, Anne smells a strange sweet odor in the cool night air. She wants to ask her father what the smell is and where they are, but everyone is moving and shouting and she knows he won't hear her. Being small, she's afraid of being lost in the crush of people.

"Women to the left! Men to the right! Line up! Line up!"

The Frank women hurry to find places in the back of a long line of female prisoners. A soldier shoves Mr. Frank toward a line of male prisoners. Anne watches him until he disappears into the crowd.

She does not know it at the time, but she will never see her father again.

Newly arrived prisoners waiting to be sorted

USHMM

A gruff voice comes over a loudspeaker and tells the new arrivals they will be required to walk two miles to reach their assigned barracks. The voice announces that trucks are parked nearby to transport anyone too old, too young, or too ill to endure the long hike.

Anne, Margot, and Mrs. Frank remain in their lines on the ramp as hundreds rush toward the waiting trucks. As soon as each vehicle is filled with people, an SS soldier drives it out of sight. Anne will later learn that none of the trucks stopped at the camp's barracks as promised.

Instead, their passengers were delivered to a different building, ordered out of the vehicles, and told to remove all clothing and shoes before they were marched into an empty, windowless room. After the young, old, and sick prisoners were packed inside, SS troops closed the doors behind them and pumped poison gas through holes in the ceiling above the prisoners' heads. The toxic fumes immediately began burning their lungs. The victims started to suffocate. Their screams quickly turned to gasping, and within fifteen minutes they were dead. Then their bodies were taken to the camp's crematoriums and burned to ashes for easy disposal. The body-burning process sent a sickly sweet smell into the surrounding night air. That's what Anne is smelling.

Anne, Margot, and Mrs. Frank, along with the other prisoners who didn't get on the trucks, are examined by doctors. SS troops and attack dogs keep guard as the doctors work. Most of the prisoners are just given a quick glance. If the doctor believes a prisoner is capable of performing strenuous physical labor, he nods for the prisoner to move to the right. If the doctor thinks a prisoner isn't fit, the prisoner is sent to the left.

Some of the people marked as unfit are sent to the camp's hospital, where German doctors will conduct bizarre medical experiments on their bodies. Most, however, are transported to the camp's gas chambers and killed. In total, more than half of the original 1,019 prisoners who arrive tonight at this new camp, Auschwitz-Birkenau, are immediately murdered.

FROM A NAME TO A NUMBER

9:30 P.M.

Anne has no reason to suspect that this new camp will be one of history's most horrible killing fields. While she knows very well about the German hatred that has put her here, she doesn't know that the German government has moved on from its earlier goals, which were to use some Jews as slaves while making the rest leave Europe. It has now decided to pursue a "Final Solution" to what it calls "the Jewish question": It will remove Judaism from the world by murdering the world's Jews. It will also murder Slavs, Gypsies, homosexuals, and other people it considers racially impure or "deviant."

Auschwitz-Birkenau (or "Auschwitz" as it's known for short) is at the heart of this plan. Originally just a prison camp, it has now grown into a complex facility made up of three primary camps, several smaller camps, and many gas chambers and crematoriums. There's also a large chemical company there, I.G. Farben, which uses some healthy Jews as slave labor. The camp has been designed to murder as efficiently as possible. The poison gas, for example, allows for the killing of hundreds of people at once. Before, the

These arrivals don't know they're being marched to a gas chamber.

Germans had to kill people one at a time with bullets, or to let health conditions become so bad that disease spread. Using a gas chamber, the Germans can murder two thousand victims at once.

Even within the camp, the extraordinary scale of the murders is not widely known. Because the Germans fear an uprising, they keep secret the true horrors of the gas chambers.

Mr. Frank, Mr. van Pels, Peter, and the other male prisoners are forced to walk to an area known as Auschwitz I, two miles from where the train arrived. Anne, Margot, and Mrs. Frank are assigned to a different section called Birkenau. First, the women are taken to a "sauna" where they are told to remove all of their clothing for "disinfection." Lice and other vermin are rampant at Birkenau, so the Germans fumigate the clothing of new prisoners to kill the bugs.

While the clothing is being treated, any female prisoners who still possess money, wedding rings, or family photos are forced to surrender the articles to the German soldiers. Then each woman is made to stand naked while guards shave her hair and tattoo a number onto her left forearm. Anne, her mother, and her sister are given numbers between A-25060 and A-25271. (Their exact numbers remain unknown.) Their hair is collected so it can be sold to companies that will use it as stuffing for mattresses and for making cloth and insulation. The women are then herded into a large room and sprayed with strong blasts of water. Then the guards use whips to force

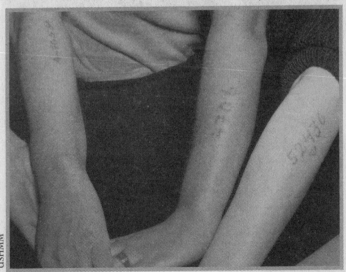

Women who survived a camp show their tattoos.

them back outside to the frigid night air. Each woman is given a thin, sack-like dress to wear.

SS soldiers are marching around their rows, looking for those too ill or too young or too old to stand during the hours it's taking the head officer to read the roll call. Anne is cold, tired, scared, hungry, and thirsty. Her arm hurts where a guard tattooed her

Women selected for slave labor, after being shaved and tattooed

new identification number. Her mother and Margot look just as exhausted. However, they know better than to let the guards see how they feel.

"Don't say you're sick!" a girl about Anne's age had warned them during the earlier march to the disinfecting sauna. "You're healthy, understand? You want to work, understand?" Though she doesn't want to work for the Nazis, Anne understands this advice. Her choice is to work or be murdered.

There's no way for us to know if she still believes at this moment that "people are really good at heart." If she does, that faith will be tested again soon. **8**

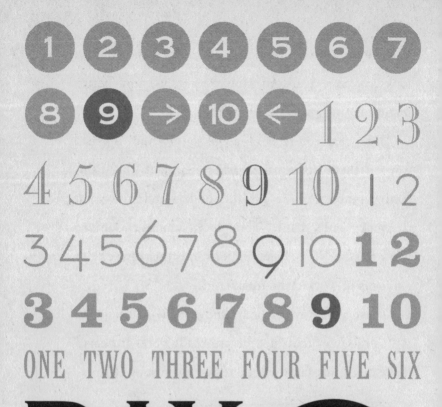

ONE TWO THREE FOUR FIVE SIX

DAY

NINE

9

OCTOBER 7,
1944

9

SECRETS AND LIES

3:30 A.M.

The morning whistle blows outside Women's Block 29 before sunrise, and one thousand female prisoners in the barrack are awakened for the workday. Anne sleeps in a narrow bunk with her mother, sister, and two other women. The bunks are straw-covered wooden shelves, stacked one above the other in rows that extend the length of the building. Most of the women have no pillows or blankets. None of them have any privacy.

Anne, Margot, and Mrs. Frank have been imprisoned at Auschwitz for four weeks, and the Nazis never allow their morning routine to change. As the women file out of the barrack's door, armed Nazi guards warily supervise their progression to the camp's latrine facility. The latrine is in a large building that contains long rows of wooden benches. The benches have hundreds of holes cut into them to accommodate the needs of as many women as possible at a single time. There are no walls to separate them while they use the restroom and no water provided for washing.

Afterward, Anne takes her soup bowl to the line where she will receive her ration of breakfast. The meal consists of some sort of brown liquid that she cannot identify, but she is hungry and eagerly extends her bowl to the server. The tiny bowl has replaced the diary as Anne's most valuable possession. She knows if it's lost or stolen, the Nazi guards will not replace it. A prisoner without a bowl, regardless of the reason, doesn't eat.

A women's barrack at Auschwitz

After drinking the soupy breakfast, all of the women are ordered to line up outside the barracks. For several hours they stand in rows as Nazi guards slowly read through the long list of their prisoner identification numbers.

This morning roll call is particularly difficult for Anne. Four weeks of hard labor and inedible food have weakened her body, and she desperately wants to sit down. Also, the skin on her left arm keeps itching today. A Nazi guard noticed her scratching it when

The "N" on the uniforms means the prisoners come from the Netherlands.

he walked past her row, and she desperately fights the urge to scratch it again in case he returns.

"Margot was close by, next to [Anne]," another prisoner remembers years later. "Anne was very calm and quiet and somewhat withdrawn. The fact that they had ended up there had affected her profoundly—that was obvious."

When roll call finally ends, the women are forced to march several miles to reach the location of their day's assigned work duties. Yesterday morning Anne and several other inmates had to hike for half an hour to a field where they spent the day hauling rocks from one large heap to another. Today they return to the same area and haul the same rocks back to their original pile.

The tedious, pointless chore is supervised by a special group of prisoners called *Kapos*. In exchange for their own safety at the camp, Kapos aid the Nazis by ensuring that ordinary prisoners like Anne obediently perform whatever tasks the SS and camp guards assign. Prisoners who refuse to conform to the Kapos' authority are immediately punished or killed.

The constant bending and lifting required by the job causes excruciating pain in Anne's arms, back, and legs. She wants to shout at the guards that it's stupid to force prisoners to spend the day moving rocks from one pile to another. She wants to plead with the Kapos to give them a few minutes' rest. But she knows neither the Germans nor the Kapos will pay heed to the logic and suffering of a Jewish girl. In fact, such rebellion might make them kill her.

At lunchtime vats of green soup are delivered to the field by other prisoners. The distribution of the meal usually occurs without conversation. This time, however, Anne sees a server whisper something to one woman in the work group. The woman looks momentarily startled by what she has been told and quickly glances in the direction of the Kapos on duty. Then she whispers something to the prisoner beside her.

When the secret finally reaches Anne, the news

is so unusual, so potentially wonderful, that she can hardly believe it's true. The *Sonderkommando* are attacking the Nazis!

The Sonderkommando ("special squad" in German) are prisoners who work for the Germans at the camp. There are nearly nine hundred of them. Their job is to convince other prisoners to willingly walk into the gas chambers, and later to drag the dead bodies out. Newly arrived prisoners are told the windowless chambers are large showers. While SS troops flood the rooms with poison gas, the Sonderkommando sort through the dying prisoners' personal belongings for valuables, which are given to the Germans. After all the victims have been killed, the Sonderkommando carry the corpses to the crematoriums for burning. Before lifting the dead bodies into the ovens, however, the Sonderkommando must remove gold from the dead prisoners' teeth and gather rings still worn by lifeless fingers.

The Sonderkommando are treated better than

other prisoners. Some welcome it, out of an animal instinct for survival. Many, however, hate the work and are filled with guilt. They do it to avoid being killed on the spot.

They also face a great risk: To keep the killings from becoming widely known, the Germans sometimes kill whole Sonderkommando crews.

Recently, members of the Birkenau Sonderkommando learned that the Nazis plan to murder them. In desperation, a few joined a secret Jewish resistance

USHMM

A gas chamber. The stains on the walls were left by poison gas.

movement operating inside the camp. The Jewish rebels have been plotting to fight the German guards for control of Auschwitz-Birkenau. Anne knew that something big might happen, but she does not know if today's excitement is part of it.

Maybe they'll kill the guards and free us, a woman near Anne says as they resume the arduous task of moving the rocks. No, another woman argues, the Sonderkommando will just get themselves killed and things will only be worse for those of us left behind.

USHMM

These crematorium ovens still have human remains inside.

After cremation, machines like this one crushed the victims' bones.

Anne wishes she could share the first woman's hope, but she fears the second is probably right. She believes it's impossible for a few prisoners, no matter how brave or determined, to overpower all of Auschwitz-Birkenau's armed Nazi guards and SS soldiers. And even if the Sonderkommando manage to kill a few of them, more will come.

Throughout the war, Anne's father had placed his hope for Jewish liberation in the hands of the advancing Allied forces. Anne wonders where the Allies are today. She bends down to lift another rock and thinks back to the secret annex in Amsterdam where she and her family had spent so many months in hiding. Was her father's map of Western Europe still hanging on the wall? Were the pins he had pushed into it after the D-Day invasion still there? Where would they place new ones, if the Frank family could magically return to the safety of those hidden rooms?

BLESSED ARE THE MEEK

7:30 P.M.

Because of the uprising, the SS soldiers and camp guards are edgy during the evening roll call of prisoners. Anne has already heard that the rebels attacked SS soldiers with hammers, axes, and sticks, then managed to blow up at least one crematorium with some sort of explosive. At roll call, however, a German officer announces that all the rebels have already been captured and executed.

Saddened by the outcome of the uprising, Anne stands silently until roll call ends. She has felt sick all day, and now her face is hot and the itching on her arm has spread to her hands and neck. She gently pushes her right sleeve up to her elbow to check the red bumps. They are larger and more numerous than before. She fights the urge to scratch them since any extra movement might draw the attention of an SS soldier.

That night, as Anne lies squeezed between her mother and Margot on the bunk in Women's Block 29, she can't sleep, despite being exhausted. She has given in to the itching of the red bumps, and now has scratched them into open sores. She knows the bumps are scabies, caused by tiny bugs that burrow under the skin of humans to lay eggs. Scratching them gives her a moment of relief, but makes her feel guilty. Scabies spreads easily in the camp's crowded, dirty conditions, and Anne knows that she risks spreading it to the women around her, including her mother and Margot.

She also knows she will be taken away from her mother and Margot if the guards see the red bumps at roll call in the morning. A prisoner in the bunk beneath her was diagnosed with scabies two days earlier. Her bumps were similar to Anne's. A Nazi doctor examined the woman and immediately ordered a guard to take her away from the barrack. No one has seen the woman since that day. ⑨

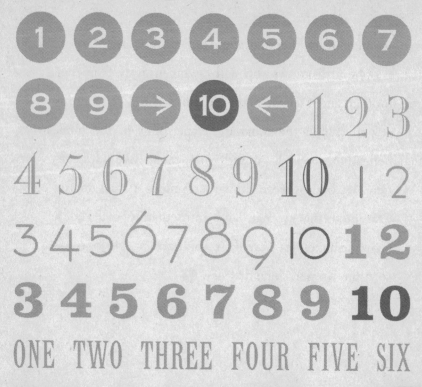

ONE TWO THREE FOUR FIVE SIX

DAY

TEN

10

MARCH

1945

"WE HAVE OUR PEACE"

Bergen-Belsen Camp, Germany. Morning.

Anne lies quietly next to Margot on the narrow bunk they share in the cold, dark barrack at their new concentration camp in Germany, where they were sent soon after the Sonderkommando uprising, about five months ago.

Like the other women housed in the room, the sisters are very ill and have been for several weeks. Anne isn't even sure of today's date. (It will never be properly recorded.) All she knows is that Margot quit eating two days ago and no longer responds to Anne's worried voice. Sometimes she awakens from a troubled sleep and cries out in pain. Anne knows Margot is dying.

A typhus epidemic has spread through the prison camp, killing thousands of prisoners in the past few weeks. Typhus is a disease transmitted by lice, and lice are rampant at Bergen-Belsen. The bugs crawl in people's bedding. They burrow in seams of clothing. They scurry across people's faces and necks.

Anne remembers her bout with scabies when they were imprisoned at Auschwitz-Birkenau and how she complained to her mother. Her mother gave up her daily food ration to make sure Anne had enough nutrients to fight the disease. Scabies is nothing compared to the deadly fever, pain, and itching Anne and Margot are experiencing from typhus. And from the terrifying moans and screams of others who are in agony because of the disease, Anne knows her symptoms will soon worsen.

What would Mother do? Anne wonders. All of the old, petty arguments with her mother seem like ancient history now. She feels immature and ashamed when she thinks of them.

Anne has never felt more alone. Her mother, whom she hasn't seen since leaving Auschwitz-Birkenau, is almost certainly dead already.

Not long after the Sonderkommando uprising, the Germans learned the Russian army was getting close to Auschwitz-Birkenau. The Nazis immediately began sending thousands of inmates to Germany, where they could not be easily liberated. Women who were considered "ill but potentially curable" were sent by train to Bergen-Belsen. Anne and Margot were among those selected. Mrs. Frank was not. Anne is sure the Germans killed her mother after the last outbound train departed.

Like Auschwitz, Bergen-Belsen is surrounded by barbed-wire fencing with points too high and sharp for prisoners to escape. Inside the fence are dozens of single-story buildings constructed over several square miles of land. The sudden arrival of so many prisoners from camps in the east has caused a complete breakdown in health conditions. The typhus epidemic can't be stopped.

Louis Tas is a Jewish teenager imprisoned at Bergen-Belsen at the same time Anne and Margot are there. The Nazis have ordered him to serve as a nurse for some of the camp's sickest people. A month earlier, Tas kept a diary of his experiences:

February 12, 1945: In the sick-bay are dirty skeletons, full of vermin, clad in rags which do not even warm them any more. What shall I do with the filthy underwear full of lice that I take off a patient? No luggage is allowed under the beds, so I carefully pick up the stuff and throw it away. This person is going to die anyway.

February 15, 1945: The huts are full of candidates for the crematorium, skeletons who only get out of bed to collect their food. There is no more tar paper on the roofs. When it rains everything gets wet, beds, blankets, luggage. In my own hut (where I don't sleep at present) there isn't even any light. Excreta lies everywhere on the camp street.

I slept in this hut one night, sharing my bed with an ill person. All day long he had been lying on his and my blanket brooding. When I as usual wrapped myself up naked into the blanket I felt lice attack me in great numbers. I had to catch and kill them with my teeth constantly, as there was no other way to get rid of them.

Bergen-Belsen camp does not have gas chambers like Auschwitz has, but it does have a small crematorium to aid guards in the disposal of dead bodies. Starvation, dehydration, and disease take the lives of so many, however, that the crematorium cannot keep pace. Thousands of corpses lie rotting, some in their bunks and others scattered around the camp's grounds.

"When we arrived," a survivor of Bergen-Belsen will later remember, "the dead were not carried away any more, you stepped over them, you fell over them if you couldn't walk. There were . . . people begging for water. They were crying, they were begging. Day and night. You couldn't escape the crying, you couldn't have escaped the praying. . . ."

Afternoon.

Margot seems to be sleeping peacefully for the moment, and Anne decides to leave the barrack in search of food. She got rid of her lice-infested clothing a few weeks ago, and now wears only a thin blanket that she wraps around herself. She climbs around Margot and unfolds her rash-covered legs over the edge of the bunk. She's weak and knows she has a fever. She fears this might be the last time she'll be strong enough to go outside.

The sky is covered with low, gray clouds when she opens the barrack's door. She steps over a dead body and heads in the direction of the fence that separates her portion of the camp from the other sections. Two men, both looking like skeletons in prisoner uniforms, are walking toward her, pulling an open wagon filled with corpses. Anne moves to one side as they pass and turns to watch them gather another body to add to their gruesome collection. One of the men picks up the dead person's feet and the other grasps the corpse's arms. They toss the body on top of those already stacked in their wagon and then drag the contraption forward a few feet to pick up another one.

Anne's walk to the barbed-wire fence is only a few meters, but it takes her frail legs several minutes to travel the short distance. Jewish prisoners held on the other side of the fence are called "exchange Jews," because the Nazis hope to trade them with the Allies in exchange for German prisoners of war. That's why

Women with typhus, just after liberation of Bergen-Belsen.

some of them have been shipped here from other camps. The exchange Jews receive better food, shelter, and care from the camp guards than prisoners like Anne and Margot do. Anne knows some of the exchange Jews will occasionally toss pieces of bread or articles of clothing over the fence, and she wants to be there if anyone does it today.

On some occasions Anne reunites with friends from her childhood who are imprisoned on the exchange side. One person she knows from her days in Amsterdam is a teenager named Hanneli Goslar. The two girls cannot see each other through the fence because the Nazis have packed straw into its holes, but they can hear each other.

Today Hanneli is able to toss a hunk of bread over the fence, but Anne does not have the strength to catch it before it falls to the ground. Another prisoner snatches it and runs away. Anne thanks Hanneli and, empty-handed, begins the difficult walk back to her barrack to check on Margot.

Margot is moaning and thrashing around on the

After evacuation, the barracks were burned to stop the disease.

bunk, and Anne waits before climbing in next to her. Margot's skin is red from her fever, but there's no cool water or medicine to help bring her temperature back to normal.

All Anne can do is lie down beside her and wrap her arms protectively around her sister. "Anne looked after [Margot] as well as she could," a friend named Lientje Brilleslijper will later remember.

Evening.

Anne tries to stay awake in case Margot needs her, but drifts into a restless sleep instead. Tonight she dreams about her parents. In her dream they are young and healthy and laughing. Then she dreams of Amsterdam on a warm summer day and of riding her bike down a sidewalk that parallels a canal. She also dreams of writing in her diary and can almost feel her pen scratching across its pages.

Someone screams and Anne jerks awake. She is afraid the sound came from Margot, but then she realizes it comes from a woman in the next bunk. The poor woman screams again and then is forever silent.

Anne refuses to leave Margot's side in the final hours of her sister's life. When her friend Lientje comes to check on them, Anne simply whispers for her not to worry. "We are together," Anne says softly, "and we have our peace."

Anne has no way of knowing that when Margot takes her final, troubled breath a few hours later, the Allied forces are only weeks away from liberating Bergen-Belsen. However, before the rescuers can reach the locked gates of the concentration camp, typhus will also take the life of fifteen-year-old Anne Frank. ⑩

1 2 3 4 5 6 7 8 9 → 10 ←

1 2 3
4 5 6 7 8 9 10 1 2
3 4 5 6 7 8 9 10 **12**
3 4 5 6 7 8 9 10

ONE TWO THREE FOUR FIVE SIX

AFTERWORD

JULY 19,
1945

LEGACY

Amsterdam. 8:15 A.M.

O n a fresh summer morning in Amsterdam, Otto Frank walks in the warm sunshine.

Anne was mistaken: He was very ill at Auschwitz, but he didn't die. Then, about six months ago, with the Soviet Union's army approaching, the Germans fled. Although they took about sixty thousand prisoners with them, the ones who were sick, like Mr. Frank, were left behind. Now, after a long journey through various parts of Europe, he's back in Amsterdam. He and Miep Gies are walking to his company's offices—to the secret annex.

Miep hears children laughing and playing somewhere out of sight, and she realizes how quickly some people have gone back to their old lives since the war ended, six weeks earlier.

She does not share her thoughts with Mr. Frank, however. Her boss walks in silence beside her, as he does every morning, lost in his feelings of grief and worry. His wife died at Auschwitz-Birkenau just three weeks before the Soviet Union's army liberated the camp. He's still looking for Anne and Margot. He hopes they're in a refugee camp, like so many other survivors. He has sent dozens of letters across Europe inquiring about his daughters' fate, but so far no one has been able to provide any information.

"They'll be coming home any day, Otto. I'm sure of it," Miep reassures him as he fumbles in his pocket for the key to the office door.

USHMM

Prisoners greet their liberators

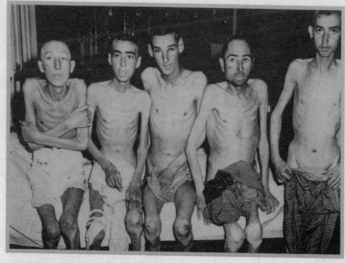

Survivors, just after liberation

Mr. Frank nods his head, pushes the door open, and steps back politely to let Miep enter the building. He is trying to remain optimistic about his daughters' eventual return, but the days keep passing without news of them, and his hope for the girls' survival is fading.

Miep organizes her desk for the workday, and Mr. Frank goes to his office. When he shuts the door, Miep knows that he'll be writing more letters today.

He already knows that Dr. Fritz Pfeffer, the dentist

that Anne had disliked, died in a camp. Mr. van Pels was murdered in the gas chambers at Auschwitz. He recently received a letter telling him that Mrs. van Pels died in April or May of 1945. Their son, Peter, is also dead. Mr. Frank had tried to convince Peter to stay behind when the Germans evacuated Auschwitz, but Peter wanted to leave. Unfortunately, the evacuation became a death march as the Germans killed prisoners who couldn't keep the pace. Because it was winter, many prisoners became sick and died.

The Germans left behind stacks of unburied corpses and eerie reminders, like this huge pile of shoes, of other victims.

Am I the only one left alive? Mr. Frank wonders. *No, it's not possible.*

He aligns a sheet of paper in his typewriter and begins tapping out the words he has written so many times to so many people over the past few weeks: "Dear Sir, I am hoping you can help me locate my daughters. . . ."

Just before lunch, the mail arrives. When the other workers go home to eat, Mr. Frank sits across from Miep at her desk and opens the letters.

After reading one, he sits very still for a moment.

"It's from the Red Cross," he says. "Margot and Anne are not coming back," he says softly. Then after a moment he stands up and politely says, "I'll be in my office."

For a long time Miep stays at her desk, unable to move or speak. After so many months of hoping and praying Anne and Margot would return, it seems impossible to suddenly know that they will not.

"I sat at my desk utterly crushed," Miep will later

remember. "Everything that has happened before, I could somehow accept. Like it or not, I had to accept it. But this, I could not accept. It was the one thing I'd been sure would not happen."

She slowly opens the desk drawer where she has hidden Anne's diary, notebooks, and the 327 loose sheets of paper she had collected from the floor of the secret annex the day the Franks, the van Pelses, and Dr. Pfeffer were arrested. Mr. Frank does not know Miep has them. She was still keeping Anne's secrets for her. "I didn't hand [Mr. Frank] Anne's writings immediately on his arrival," she says later, "[because] I still hoped . . . Anne would come back."

Miep hadn't even touched them herself. Now she does—the nearest thing she can do to holding Anne and Margot again.

She gathers the diary and other papers and goes to Mr. Frank's closed door. When he doesn't answer her knock, she gently turns the knob. Mr. Frank is sitting at his desk with his head bowed between his hands.

"Here is your daughter," Miep whispers. "Anne's legacy to you."

She carefully places the precious items on the desk in front of him. Mr. Frank stares at them but says nothing. Miep quietly leaves the room.

As he looks down at the checkerboard cover of the diary, a pain grips his stomach. He can see Anne sitting on her bed in the annex, her back against the wall of movie star photographs, intensely writing her thoughts on its pages.

His fingertips move across the fabric cover, but it will be months before he has the strength to read her words. Until he speaks with Lientje Brilleslijper, who confirms that Anne and Margot are dead, he'll hold on to the hope that the Red Cross made a mistake.

When he finally does read the diary, Anne and Margot and his wife will come alive for him again. He'll then have a new mission: help Anne tell the story she wanted to tell. It won't be the same as survival, but, maybe, it will be as enduring. ⸺

June 12, 1929: Annelies Marie Frank is born in Frankfurt, Germany.

January 30, 1933: After astonishing gains for the Nazi Party in the parliamentary elections of the previous year, Adolf Hitler is made head of the German government.

Spring 1933: The Nazis begin large-scale arrests of political enemies and declare a boycott of Jewish businesses and professionals. Books by Jewish authors and other newly declared "enemies" of Germany are burned. Later, all other political parties are declared illegal.

Summer 1933: The Franks flee to the Netherlands.

January 1934: The German government begin programs to murder and sterilize people it declares "unfit."

Summer 1935: The German government begins to pass laws against Jews.

March 12, 1938: Germany invades Austria.

November 9–10, 1938: The German government backs *Kristallnacht*, in which mobs attack Jews and Jewish businesses, schools, and synagogues.

March–September 1939: Germany invades Czechoslovakia and then Poland. The Second World War begins.

May 1940: Germany invades the Netherlands.

June 12, 1942: For her thirteenth birthday, Anne receives the autograph book she uses as a diary.

July 5, 1942: Margot receives a letter requiring her to report the next day for imprisonment in a labor camp.

July 6, 1942: The Franks abandon their apartment and move to the secret annex.

July 13, 1942: The van Pels family joins the Frank family in the annex.

November 16, 1942: Dr. Fritz Pfeffer joins the Frank and van Pels families in the annex. He and Anne share a bedroom.

March 28, 1944: Prompted by a radio broadcast by the Dutch government in exile, Anne decides to improve her diary for publication.

June 6, 1944: The Allied Forces fighting Germany land in France to begin the major offensive that will end the war.

August 4, 1944: An anonymous caller tells the German police how to find the annex. Anne and the other residents of the annex, as well as the friends who helped them hide, are arrested.

August 8, 1944: The Jewish prisoners are transferred to the Westerbork camp.

September 3, 1944: The last train leaves the Netherlands for Auschwitz-Birkenau. All eight residents of the secret annex are on it.

October 1944: Anne and Margot are sent to the Bergen-Belsen camp.

January 6, 1945: Mrs. Frank dies at Auschwitz-Birkenau.

January 27, 1945: The Russian army liberates Auschwitz-Birkenau, freeing Otto Frank.

March 1945: Anne and Margot die in a typhus epidemic at Bergen-Belsen.

May 7, 1945: Germany surrenders.

Fall 1945: Otto Frank learns his daughters died at Bergen-Belsen. Miep Gies gives him the diary she has been holding for Anne's return.

June 25, 1947: Anne's diary is published, in the original Dutch, in Amsterdam.

1952: The first English translation of Anne's diary is published.

NOTES AND SELECTED BIBLIOGRAPHY

Barnouw, David, and Gerrold Van Der Strom, eds. *The Diary of Anne Frank: The Critical Edition*. New York: Doubleday, 1989. Copyright © 1986 by Anne Frank-Fons, Basel, Switzerland, for all texts by Anne Frank. English translation copyright © 1989 by Doubleday, a division of Random House, Inc.

Frank, Otto, and Mirjam Pressler, eds. *The Diary of a Young Girl: The Definitive Edition*. New York: Doubleday, 1995. Copyright © 1991 by Anne Frank-Fons, Basel, Switzerland, for all texts by Anne Frank. English translation copyright © 1995 by Doubleday, a division of Random House, Inc.

Gies, Miep. *Anne Frank Remembered*. New York: Simon and Schuster, 1987.

Lee, Carol Ann. *Roses From the Earth: A Biography of Anne Frank*. New York: Penguin Books, 2000.

Muller, Melissa. *Anne Frank: The Biography*. New York: Henry Holt and Company, 1998.

Westra, Hans. Introduction to *Inside Anne Frank's House*. New York: Overlook Duckworth, 2004.

Websites of special interest:
Anne Frank Center:
   http://www.annefrank.com
Anne Frank House/Anne Frank Museum Amsterdam:
   http://www.annefrank.org
Jewish Virtual Library:
   http://www.jewishvirtuallibrary.org
United States Holocaust Memorial Museum:
   http://www.ushmm.org

NOTES

p. iii, "I come from a people": speech delivered January 27, 1998.
Cited at the Jewish Virtual Library website, accessed May 7, 2008:
http://www.jewishvirtuallibrary.org/jsource/Quote/BauerHolo.html

p. 1, "IBM": See Edwin Black's *IBM and the Holocaust*. New York: Crown Books, 2001.

p. 17, "After May 1940": *Diary, Definitive Edition,* June 20, 1942.

p. 24, "It's the council's responsibility": *Justiz und NS-Verbrechen* ("Nazi Crimes on Trial"), Band XXV, Lfd.Nr.645. Website, accessed February 11, 2008:
http://www1.jur.uva.nl/junsv/Excerpts/64512.htm

p. 26, "Jews were required to": *Diary, Definitive Edition,* June 20, 1942.

p. 33, "I put in": *Diary, Critical Edition,* translation C, July 8, 1942.

p. 34, "We got sympathetic looks": *Diary, Critical Edition,* translation C, July 9, 1942.

p. 38, "No one would ever guess": *Diary, Critical Edition,* translation C, July 9, 1942.

p. 50, "History cannot be written": Lee, 142.

p. 58, "I *know* that I can write": *Diary, Definitive Edition,* April 5, 1944.

p. 64, "Oh, not my diary": *Diary, Definitive Edition,* April 11, 1944.

p. 65, "Now we are lost": *Diary, Critical Edition,* translation C, April 11, 1944.

p. 66, "During that night": *Diary, Critical Edition,* translation C, April 11, 1944.

p. 66, "When someone comes in": *Diary, Critical Edition,* translation C, December 24, 1943.

p. 69, "We have been pointedly reminded": *Diary, Critical Edition,* translation C, April 11, 1944.

p. 72, "This is D-day": *Diary, Critical Edition,* translation C, June 6, 1944.

p. 74, "in spite of everything": *Diary, Critical Edition,* translation C, July 15, 1944.

p. 80, "You can't imagine": Schnabel, Ernst, *The Footsteps of Anne Frank.* London: Pan Books, 1976; 115–117. Quoted in Lee, 151.

p. 85, "We were together": Schnabel, 117, quoted in Lee, 155.

p. 98, "I think of darkness": reminiscence of Frieda Menco in Westra, 197.

p. 115, "Margot was close by": reminiscence of Ronnie Goldenstein-van Cleef in Lindwer, Willy, *The Last Seven Months of Anne Frank*. New York: Pantheon, 1991; 186. Quoted in Lee, 174.

p. 128, "In the sick-bay": Vogel, Loden (pseudonym of Dr. Louis Tas), *Diary from a Camp* (1965). Via website: "What Was It Like at Bergen-Belsen?" ScrapbookPages.Com. 2002, accessed Feb. 15, 2008: http://www.scrapbookpages.com/BergenBelsen/BergenBelsen07. html

p. 130, "When we arrived": reminiscence of Alice Lok Cahana, United States Holocaust Memorial Museum, "Personal Histories." United States Holocaust Memorial Museum website, accessed Feb, 15, 2008: http://www.ushmm.org/museum/exhibit/online/phistories/ phi_camps_arrival_uu.htm

p. 134, "Anne looked after [Margot]": reminiscence of Lientje Brilleslijper-Jaladati, "Memories," in Hellwig, Joachim, and Gunther Deicke, *Ein Tagebuch für Anne Frank*. Berlin: Verlag der Nation, 1959. Quoted in Lee, 191.

p. 135, "We are together": reminiscence of Lientje Brilleslijper-Jaladati, "Memories," in Hellwig, Joachim, and Gunther Deicke, *Ein Tagebuch für Anne Frank*. Berlin: Verlag der Nation, 1959. Quoted in Lee, 191.

p. 138, "They'll be coming home" [and other dialogue from this scene]: Gies, 233–235.

PHOTO CREDITS

The photos on the following pages are copyright of the United States Holocaust Memorial Museum (USHMM) and are reprinted here by permission of the USHMM: v (star, photo of Anne), vi (Westerbork), vii (all photos), 11, 23, 27, 81, 86, 88, 89, 96, 97, 100, 101, 105, 107, 108, 113, 114, 118, 119, 120, 132, 133, 139, 140, 141.

The views or opinions expressed in this book, and the context in which